AF593460

Hello
Job!

ALISON
CRAIG

Hello Job!

How to psych up, suit up, & show up!

BLUE MONARCH PRESS

Tempe, AZ | BlueMonarchPress.com

BLUE MONARCH PRESS
60 E Rio Salado Parkway
Suite 900
Tempe, AZ 85281

BlueMonarchPress.com

For special quantity pricing, please contact
Blue Monarch Press at 1-877-242-1911 or Care@BlueMonarchPress.com.

Edited by Gwyn Nichols
Designed by Design Corp
Manufactured in the United States of America

Library of Congress Preassigned Control Number: 2010900496

ISBN 978-0-9844131-0-2 (paperback)

"Ask, and it will be given to you,
seek, and you will find,
knock, and it will be opened to you."

Matthew 7:7 NASB

Foreword

Alison Craig has a passion to use her God-given talents as an Image Consultant to be a powerful element in assisting people to find jobs using the Phoenix First Workforce.

As a major inspiration and foundation of the Workforce team, Alison brings her fresh perspective from a servant's heart to encourage people to look their best, be their best, and succeed!

Within this book, Alison details how a job seeker can sharpen your image not only in how you dress and groom, but also with important interview skills.

I highly recommend this book and know that it will be a valuable tool in helping people say, "Hello, Job!"

We are blessed to have her.

—*Pastor Tommy Barnett*
Phoenix First Assembly

Acknowledgements

Thank you to all the many people who have helped get this book to you, the readers' hands: David, Daniel, Gwyn, John and Dan, Mom and Dad, and most importantly, God. Thank you to Pastors Tommy and Luke Barnett for allowing and encouraging the creation of Phoenix First Workforce. Thank you for all of the help and support.

Dedication

To all the job seekers. May you find your God-given careers in His timing for your lives.

The origins of this book began from a servant's heart. Through my personal experience with Phoenix First Workforce, I have seen many job seekers come and go. The ones who find success, who find their jobs quickly, are the ones who have followed the steps in this book. Congratulations on taking a wonderful step in the right direction. I only wish I could know how this book will help you personally. I know this is a tough time, not only for you, but for your family, loved ones, and all who rely upon you. Always remember:

You are not alone.

You are enough.

You are fully capable.

You are wonderful just the way that you are.

You are loved.

Sincerely,
Alison Craig

Contents

Part One: Psyche Up

1	It Starts with an "Up" Look	3
2	Are You Sabotaging Yourself?	5
3	_________________'s Job	7
4	"Hello, Job!"	9
5	Has the Media Set You Up to Fail?	11
6	The 3 Impressions You Need to Make	15
7	Five Secrets for a Successful Interview	17
8	So Who Are You, Anyway?	19

Part Two: Suit Up

9	We Saw That	25
10	The FIRST First Impression	27
11	What Do Your Clothes Say about You?	33
12	Interview Dress Basics	35
13	Colors Speak. What's Your Message?	37

SUIT UP FOR WOMEN

14	The New Rules for Women's Business Dress	47
15	Look Five Pounds Thinner Today	45
16	Look Great in the Body You Have, Ladies	49
17	Women's Interview Outfits	57

SUIT UP FOR MEN

18 Why Men Have It Easy 61

19 Look Great in the Body You Have, Guys 64

20 Men's Business Dress 67

21 Overcoming Preconceptions 71

Part Three: Show Up

22 Leave Your Baggage Behind 75

23 The View from the Other Side of the Desk 81

24 Want a No-Panic Interview? 85

25 Is Your Body Language Ratting You Out? 89

26 Mouth Don't Fail Me Now 91

27 Find Your Job Sooner 95

28 Hello, Job, at Last! 97

PART ONE

CHAPTER 1

It Starts with an "Up" Look

Many job seekers have told me that they feel as though they are in a war zone, trying to figure out which way to go. They feel lost. All they want to do is find their target, a job, so that they can go home. They inspired *Hello, Job!*

There are many great books on the market that can teach you to write a résumé or answer interview questions, and we do touch on those things, but our main focus here is on how to make the most positive, impactful, and lasting impression at your interview. That means you're going into that conversation totally prepared to Psyche Up, Suit Up, and Show Up. You have a positive outlook, we've done a makeover on your image, you know what to say, and you're ready to land that job.

People hire those they can relate to—they'll be working together after all—and sometimes you need to be a chameleon. I am here to teach you how to do that, yet stay true to who you really are.

That doesn't mean that it will be quick, easy, or painless, but you are no longer in this alone. With this handbook to encourage and guide you, you'll soon be saying, "Hello, Job!"

CHAPTER 2

Are You Sabotaging Yourself?

Looking for a job can be a quick way to face all your insecurities. Are you smart enough? Friendly enough? Will people like you? It can make you feel as though you're back in elementary school, hoping to be picked for the team. No one wants to be picked last. And sometimes, just to make sure you don't feel so bad about being picked last, you might even unwittingly sabotage yourself before anyone else has a chance to reject you.

Please don't take that personally; we've all sabotaged ourselves at some point, and we don't want to look at that either. It is way easier to blame others. We don't have to live with all the "others," but we do live with ourselves. It's tough to realize that the insecurities that you thought you had so happily left behind at school are still living inside you and are rearing their ugly heads now!

So how can you stop all the self-sabotage, especially the insecurities that talk to you all the time? Well, first off, admit that you're human, so it's going to happen. Secondly, notice the root. It's just fear—regular, everyday, garden-variety fear! Fear is what is stopping you. And what is fear? My favorite definition of F.E.A.R. is False Evidence Appearing Real.

And why are we listening to something that is false, a lie? We do this because we are too stressed out to even take a moment, stop, breathe, and consider the situation at hand. So stop. Breathe. And realize that you are fully capable of handling the job or interview at hand.

And guess what? You are good enough. Think about it: most people don't apply for a job for which they have absolutely zero qualifications. And that dreaded fear that no one will like you is wrong as well. People will like you. Are they going to be your new best friends? Maybe, maybe not, and yes, a few people won't love you as much as they should, but that is okay. There is a great job for you, on the right team. Your first job is to go out and find it!

When you are job searching and are in the interview process, you might sometimes feel like you're seven years old again, rather scared and inadequate. Remember then that the fear is a lie. It is False Evidence Appearing Real. In any sport, you'll probably strike out a few times, but your next turn is available as soon as you're willing to jump back into the game. The choice is always yours. You are never a quitter unless you refuse to try again. You will be chosen. You will end up on a great team.

CHAPTER 3

___________'s Job

So whose name did you put in the blank? Was it yours? Or was it somebody else's? There is a job out there with your name on it. With that said, finding your job is not as easy as calling up some 1-800 number and saying, "Hi. This is Alison. What is my next job, please?" If only it could be that easy! The good news is that you are not alone.

Finding a new career can be challenging, no matter what the job market is like in any particular year. The advantage of job seeking during an economic downturn is that there is plenty of free help out there for job seekers. So if you want help polishing your résumé or you want to learn a new skill, there are plenty of government funded and nonprofit options out there for you. You can even begin a new career. What a great time to expand your knowledge and your skills. You now have a golden opportunity to take a new path and find the career that suits you, in a new arena where your talents can make a greater contribution.

So, yes, searching for a new job isn't often fun. Maybe you didn't choose to go looking for a job right now. Maybe this has been a terrible shock. But since you are looking, this can definitely be the catalyst for creating the life you desire and deserve.

I'd like you to consider how many things begin as simple seeds: oak trees, corn, roses. It's hard to know what a seed really is until it is planted in fertile soil, watered and nourished, and begins to grow.

And how do most seeds arrive at their destination? Quite often, not by choice, but by chance. Maybe it's a wind. That forceful—sometimes violent—act catapults the seed from where it began to a place it can grow. So, yes, job searching is not always pleasant, and yes, it can sometimes feel violent, but when all is said and done, you will be planted in a place where your true talents, passion, and desires can be realized.

CHAPTER 4

"Hello, Job!"

Say that out loud for a second: "Hello, Job!" Don't you just smile? We all want to be able to say those words. Most of us never said them before, but now we would love to.

Do you go into each interview with that mindset? The mindset that believes this is your job already, and that the interview is a formality. This is not to say that you should be cocky or arrogant. You should show the interviewer great respect and confidence. If this job is right for your talents, your personality, and your needs, then it is already your job; they just don't know it yet. That's why they are interviewing. They are looking for you.

So begin to say, "Hello, Job!" as you submit your résumé and prepare for your interviews. Remember your job is waiting for you. You are the answer to your future employer's prayer.

CHAPTER 5

Has the Media Set You Up to Fail?

In the movies, job seeking is often played for humor, and in almost any interview scene, the interviewer is portrayed as the opponent. And since a great interview is neither comedy nor tragedy, you won't often see positive and effective interview skills demonstrated on film. Most people never get any type of interview coaching or preparation before they go into that interview, and you might not even realize that those negative expectations planted by the media could influence how your interview goes.

My favorite example of this can be found in the movie *The Wedding Singer* with Adam Sandler. In this particular scene, Adam Sandler's character, Robbie Hart, is broken. He lost the girl and just wants to get her back. He has been told to go get a job and make lots of money.

So Robbie thinks about where he could get a lot of money—the bank. He figures the bank can give him money. He doesn't have any banking skills, and his focus is only on the money and getting a lot of it. Needless to say, the interview doesn't go well, and Robbie abruptly ends it himself, saying, "I didn't get the job, did I?"

So let's review what Robbie did right and what he could have done better. Robbie did do a few positive things. He was dressed for success—at least according to the expectations of the 1980s. And he was honest.

Here's where this character sabotaged himself:

- He didn't prepare and research the company he was interviewing with.
- He wasn't qualified for the position.
- He focused on himself and his needs, rather than how he could help the company.
- He ended the interview himself, never giving the interviewer a chance to speak. Maybe the interviewer could have suggested a different position within the organization.
- He saw the interviewer as the enemy not the ally.

In the movies, you'll often see that example of evil rivalry between the job interviewer and the job seeker. It creates more drama—or comedy. And yes, situations like that can occur, but they are not the norm in real life. Whoever is interviewing you—be it the head of Human Resources or the owner of the company—that person is not your enemy. This person is anxiously looking for the best person for the job. When you are that person, you make your interviewer's day. Now they can get back to their real job, and even have you to help them do it.

You, as the interviewee, should simply be honest and join the interviewer in finding the best person for the job as well.

It's great when that person is you, but if it isn't, let them know that as well. Think about how much they would appreciate hearing, "I can tell I'm not the right fit for this position," Or "I don't have that much experience in that area. I would have to learn such and such." Honesty is quickly becoming a lost art. So by being honest, you not only save yourself the embarrassment of being shown as a fraud, but you also become positively memorable and likeable.

Lastly, don't suddenly end the relationship altogether like Adam Sandler's character did. Your honesty about what you can (and can't) do might even lead you to another position with that company. And if not, at least you were honest, and established a warm and open relationship with the interviewer. You never know where having friends like that could lead.

Another great film example of an interview gone wrong can be seen in *You, Me, and Dupree*. Owen Wilson's character, Randolph Dupree, goes on an interview. Instead of being interested in meeting the needs of the company, Dupree is more interested in what holidays he will have off. He goes on and on, listing both obvious and obscure holidays he's expecting to celebrate.

Approach your interviews knowing that you and the interviewer are actually on the same side, finding the right fit between the job and the employee. Be honest and friendly. Put the company's requirements before your own and you will make an amazing positive impression.

CHAPTER 6

The 3 Impressions You Need to Make

You make three impressions on the people you meet: their first impression of you, their last impression of you, and the lasting impression you leave with them. In business, these 3 Impressions are crucial to growing and maintaining a thriving and progressive business; while job seeking, making a negative impression won't just cost you the sale, it could cost you the job.

We have all heard a lot about first impressions because they mean a lot, but in a competitive job market, you aren't just going to be interviewing once, but typically two or three times! These companies want to make sure that you are the real deal and not just putting on an act for one time. And it is in this situation where the last and lasting impressions come into play.

Let me define those terms for you because they are not as well known as the first impression. The last impression is the most recent impression someone has of you. So for example, how you end your interview is the last impression the interviewer has of you.

The lasting impression is a combination of everything someone knows or perceives about you. In the example of a job interview, the lasting impression of you is what the interviewer has thought of you through your résumé, the first few moments he/she has met you, and all the other times they have met or seen you.

I would like to stress the point of being seen. Many times when you go into a job interview, you think it is just you, the secretary, and other applicants who might notice you, but you don't know until it is too late that the other person in the elevator is your interviewer. Maybe their offices look out over the parking lot and they saw you arrive and walk in.

That lasting impression is a total combination of everything that the interviewer knows about you.

I know this can all sound quite mean and calculating, but it really isn't. We all do this to everyone we meet. It just happens so quickly that most of us don't take the time to be consciously aware of it.

View the interview process as though you are dating. You wouldn't decide to marry someone from meeting them for twenty minutes or less—plus a little bit you read about them. Now doesn't that seem silly? Of course, it does.

Well, in a fierce job market, companies don't have to accept the first qualified candidate anymore. The companies can take their time to get to know you—see who you really are, and what you're really like.

This isn't just good for them, but for you as well. Many of these companies are looking for long-term employees who will be happy and productive. They don't want to be refilling the position in six months to a year. As much as it feels like a frustrating, long, and arduous process, it is really for the best for all.

So how can you make positive impressions everywhere that you go? By understanding that these impressions are always occurring, and by always being prepared to put the best light on your positive attributes.

CHAPTER 7

Five Secrets for a Successful Interview

Here are my keys for feeling more relaxed, appearing your best, and being more confident, which all leads to a successful interview:

1. **Prepare.** Research the position you are applying for. Understand the company's values, mission, and culture. Also, learn about the business etiquette for your region.

2. **Polish.** Take time to plan your interview wardrobe and polish your appearance. (I'll be explaining that in great detail.) Make sure that your look fits you, the company, and the position you are interviewing for.

3. **Practice.** Practice your interviewing skills and be prepared for the likely questions, especially that dreaded opener, "Tell me a little bit about yourself."

4. **Posture.** Be aware of your posture and stand tall. Proper body language sends the right message to others, and raises your own self-confidence.

5. **Positive.** Be positive no matter how you feel the interview is going, and stay positive throughout the job seeking process.

What ties these keys together? Purpose. You can't just blindly shoot at a job, or at anything in life, and expect to hit your mark. So take the time to research the companies you are applying to, create your appearance on purpose, practice answering questions and carrying yourself with self-confident posture, and intentionally keep a positive attitude. As my good friend Daniel Gonzalez, head of the Phoenix First Workforce, always says, "Finding a job is your job until you get a job."

CHAPTER 8

So Who Are You, Anyway?

Who are you? Sounds like a simple question, doesn't it? Have you already answered it in your own mind? Or is your mind blank, thinking, "I don't actually know!"

Most people really don't know who they are, or at least aren't ready to introduce themselves in a concise and compelling way. And if you don't know who you are, how is anyone else going to understand you? This can be quite detrimental when job seeking for many reasons.

First off, by not knowing who you are, you limit yourself to looking only at jobs that you have always done. If you have been waiting tables, then you only look for similar positions. If you have only been a lower level manager, you only look at positions in the traditional manager sense. Besides limiting your job search leads, it also limits you. It keeps you stagnating, instead of reaching and growing into your true potential.

Secondly, if you know who you are, you can describe yourself successfully in your interviews. It's a skill to honestly know who you are. You are with yourself all the time, but maybe you don't really notice what sets you apart. Maybe it's second nature that you always show up ten minutes early everywhere you go, and being dependable is a characteristic that most companies are desperately looking for. So if you don't take time to remember who you are and verbalize those qualities, you will most likely miss some of your most wonderful and valuable traits.

So complete the following list. Take a few moments to honestly reflect on these topics, asking, "Who are you?" By doing so, you will not only remember what you truly desire and want, you will also rediscover all the positive things that make you, you. And that boost to your self-esteem can make all the difference in the impressions you make and in your ability to take on a new challenge.

1. What I most enjoy doing.
2. When I am most happy.
3. What I would be in an ideal world—and why.
4. The qualities I most admire about myself.
5. The qualities I most admire in others.
6. The things I will never do.
7. An area I'd like to improve in.
8. What I feel most confident doing.
9. What I would love to do or be, except that I feel I need to learn more.

Once you have completed your list, you can use this information to help you move forward, and end up with a job that you love at a company that loves you back. Here's an example.

Sarah is out of work. She has worked in the customer service field, answering phones for a large company ever since college. Even though Sarah has a degree in Fine Arts, she has never used it. Sarah likes helping others, and working in a call center is something that she knows, but now Sarah is finding it difficult to find a call center customer service position. What is she to do? Here is Sarah's list:

1. I most enjoy doing anything creative.
2. I am most happy when I am helping others.
3. In an ideal world, I would be a fashion designer because I love fabrics and colors.
4. The qualities I most admire about myself are that I am dependable, honest, and hard working.
5. The qualities I most admire in others are their boldness and fearless attitudes.
6. The things I will never do are anything illegal or immoral.
7. An area I'd like to improve is overcoming my shyness.
8. I feel most confident helping others.
9. I would love to be a designer, but I feel that I need to learn more.

So in Sarah's example, she realized that she enjoys people, loves serving others, is dependable, and loves being creative. She is a bit shy, but is willing to overcome it. So how will knowing this help her find the job of her dreams?

Now Sarah can see objectively that there is so much more that she actually enjoys besides her work in a call center. Sarah could also look for positions in the fashion or design fields, as well as in customer service. She could easily apply for jobs such as these: sales clerk at a clothing store; personal assistant to an interior designer, architect, graphic designer, or jewelry designer; sales associate in a fabric store or design trade showroom; secretary for an alteration or upholstery shop. She could even think about applying for a customer service or sales associate position at a furniture store. Now that she knows who she is, Sarah can broaden her job search.

And yes, she is qualified for all of those positions. She has customer service experience, telephone experience, a degree in fine arts, creativity, and a desire to help others. She is willing to overcome her shyness and has even done that in her customer service job. To top it off, she is dependable and honest. She would be perfect for any of these jobs, and those employers would be fortunate to find her.

Besides broadening your job search beyond what you have been doing, and giving yourself some additional viable options, you can now see clearly and plainly, in black and white, what qualities about yourself you want to highlight in your résumé and in an interview. And even though a weakness could be viewed as a negative, when you are willing to overcome it, you can let the interviewer know that you are growing in that way as well.

Maybe this exercise pointed out a job you'd love and are qualified for, but you don't feel you have enough experience. A great way to get started is to find a place to volunteer at doing that work while you are job searching. This way you strengthen your skill set and your self-esteem, and maybe even your connections, and next thing you know, you are experienced enough.

So now that you know who you are, let's suit up for the search.

PART TWO

CHAPTER 9

We Saw That

Not to make you paranoid, but we did see that. People all around you are watching you. Who are these people? Are they perfect strangers? Could this be your next employer or a person who knows your next employer?

We've already talked about how important it is to make a positive first, last, and lasting impression. Various studies have concluded that we form that first impression of someone very quickly; some say within the first thirty seconds, and others say it's only two. My guess is that we register the impression within those two seconds and then it may take up to thirty seconds to decide what we'll do about it. However long it takes, it's practically instantaneous.

If you stop to think about it, you'll remember you have experienced this. You have seen someone walk into a room and immediately thought something about them: either you wanted to get to know them, or you decided you didn't. Maybe you've noticed that others size you up just as quickly. How long does it take you to guess a person's age, perceived level of success, personality, competence, and trustworthiness? Remember that this isn't about you, and it's nothing personal. Our two-second prejudgment is pure instinct. It is built into our psyches to protect us.

And then, because we're human, we also take it personally when others prejudge us.

Think about the last time you went to the grocery store, and you were looking for a piece of fruit. Didn't you choose that fruit by its appearance? We judge people in the same light. We first judge with our eyes before we know anything about anyone. Rather than take this personally, I want to help you use this aspect of human nature to your advantage.

Sometimes your first impression can be planned. You have a job interview or a networking luncheon. You dress up and prepare to make that important first impression.

However, here's the catch: how many first impressions happen without consulting your calendar, when you least expect them? Everywhere you go, you're making a first impression on someone. And while you're finding your job, you're completely aware of how much those impressions mean to your success.

Besides working with my regular clients who are usually business owners, I also volunteer to help job seekers learn these vital skills that no one really teaches any more. Unlike business owners, job seekers really do have only one chance to make that positive first impression. No redo here. And you never know when or where you might meet the person who can open the door to your next job. So let me show you how to be prepared for that first impression, no matter where it happens.

In an interview situation, especially, you already know that you want to be sharp and chic. I want you to be the apple they choose, that pristine and polished apple. I want the potential employers to give you a chance over all the other job seekers, and if that was only because of your polished professional look, then so be it. Remember, this is just instinctual human nature.

CHAPTER 10

The FIRST First Impression

When I say "first impression," do you think of your clothes? I hope you did, because I have plenty more to say about that.

But even before an employer meets you, that very first impression will often be your résumé. The words you use, the font style, format—every little piece adds up to making a positive impression on the page, one that can lead to the next step in a whole career. So to get you to that successful personal interview, first let's make a great impression with one awesome résumé.

Writing a résumé is like putting a puzzle together. It doesn't require a lot of creativity. The basic shape is always the same, a rectangle. But how the pieces—your employment history—fit together is what make your résumé stand out from the rest.

First, be clear about the position you are applying for and the company's values and mission statement. What do they stand for? Does that match what you stand for?

Next, stop and ask yourself if you have been as careful in the quality and polish of your résumé as you are with your appearance. You need to understand your résumé and what it means. These days, if you have fudged any little bit here or there, you will most likely get found out.

YOUR TWO RÉSUMÉS

You should have at least two résumés: your basic job-seeking résumé and a more detailed interview résumé. Think of the first one as a teaser. It is a simple one-page résumé tailored to the specific job position and company you are applying for.

Yes, you read that correctly: you need to tweak your résumé for each job you apply for.

Now tweaking is not lying. Tweaking is honestly tailoring the way you describe your skill set to highlight your relevance to a particular job.

If you are applying for a managerial job, you will want to highlight that you are a good leader and independent thinker, whereas if you are applying for a customer service position, you will want to emphasize that you are friendly and approachable, and you can help the company increase their bottom line.

Your second résumé also should be tailored for each job interview as well, but this résumé can be a bit longer and go into more detail about how you have helped your previous employers succeed. You'll also focus on how you can help the new company. If you keep your focus on helping their company, you will stand out in a positive light from your competition.

Now that we understand the two types of résumés any job seeker should have, how should it look and what should it say?

FROM THE TOP

Let's start at the top of your résumé, your contact information. Make sure that you have a working phone number with working voice mail. Your voice mail message should be friendly, warm, and professional. No "Leave a message, dude."

If you think that your current telephone number will change in a month or two, then ask a friend if you can put their phone number on your résumé. This is crucial because some jobs aren't placing immediately and are taking a month or two to invite you to interviews.

Once your friend agrees, ask to change the voice mail to something neutral, but professional like, "Hi, you have reached 123-4567.

Please leave your name, number, and a brief message, and we will make sure to call you back shortly. Thanks and have a great day."

A message like this is simple enough for both parties. Just make sure that your friend gives you the messages or that there is a way to retrieve them yourself.

There are even telephone numbers and voicemails available through the government for job seekers. So check with your local social services or Workforce office for more information.

With that said, make sure that your e-mail address is also professional. If your current e-mail is cute, trendy, or is not your name, create a new one for yourself and your résumé. You can get a free email address at yahoo, gmail, or a variety of other sites. Try to get your name if possible with minimal numbers or underscores. If your name is difficult to spell, use your initial. Eliminate any reason that could make it difficult for the employer to contact you.

THE MIDDLE

Summarize your best qualities, and list at least your three most recent jobs. Make sure to highlight your strengths, such as your long employment at a job, the way you increased profits at that company, or any awards or recognition you received.

The words you choose are key, especially in this day and age of online submitted résumés. You can no longer choose a special paper to reflect who you are.

Make sure to vary your phrases without bland repetitions. Choose words that actually describe the quality person you are, not a lot of buzzwords that don't mean anything. So instead of saying that you have "Excellent customer service skills," mention a specific example of great customer service skills like, "Assisted clients with product selection and was voted number one associate three years straight." This shows how you did provide customer service, and that you were successful with your previous employer. And yes, while being descriptive, you must still limit yourself to a one-page résumé. Anything more is just too much, and most likely won't get read.

For samples of résumés that Phoenix First Workforce has used with great success, download them free from the website at HelloJobBook.com.

Make sure to check out the headers, overall layout, font style, and type of information included. These résumé templates work great when applying online because your answers and key words are all ready for you.

PUTTING THE PUZZLE TOGETHER

Now when it comes to the layout, the look of your résumé is key. You want to give the interviewer enough information to call you for a personal interview, but not so much that they think they already understand the entire situation.

You'll use a simpler résumé style for a customer service or manual labor type of position, or a more complex résumé style for a management position or other situation where you have so much quality information, it's hard to get it all on one page. If you are suffering from the too much information syndrome, make sure that you are giving the interviewer the key information to describe why you are the best person for their job.

As the times change and we become a more technology driven society, so does the way we write and submit résumés. Some large companies who still allow you to mail or fax your résumé in (rather than applying online) actually use scanning software to store their résumés. If you think the position you are applying for could be a company like this, call them and ask if they scan the résumés they receive. If they do, then you will want to follow these two main tips:

1. Don't use columns or bullets. Just list the summary in paragraph form with key phrases separated by commas, and be sure to include all the key words mentioned in the job posting.

2. Don't include an objective. It's redundant when it's accompanied by a cover letter, and it could rule you out if the scanning pulls up your résumé for a different job when your qualifications match.

Even if you're submitting your résumé online, when you interview, you will want to have a printed version of your résumé. Try a nice linen or watermarked paper in a bright white. Avoid colors; they can look dated and can give an immature feel to your résumé. Make your résumé as crisp and clean as your own appearance should be.

CALLING CARDS

When applying for white-collar jobs, it is important to create a business card or calling card with your name, contact information, education, and skill set on it. This way you can pass out your information when you run into people you know who may have a connection for you without having to forward everyone your résumé.

Besides being great for when you are out and about, these calling cards also come in handy at your interview. You are able to exchange cards with your interviewer. Calling cards can be one more added layer to creating a polished and professional look that lands you the job. They also make you a perceived equal with your interviewer, which is so important during the interview process.

CHAPTER 11

What Do Your Clothes Say about You?

We all think we know the basics on how to look good. Well, some of us do and some of us don't. If we all knew how to look amazing every time we left our homes, there wouldn't be so many shows and magazines touting articles with titles like "Worst dressed" and "What were they thinking?" You know these people on the worst dressed list didn't plan to be on it. They thought they looked great. A fashion faux pas can happen daily, and no one wants a fashion disaster on their interview day.

Along with impeccable grooming, a current and flattering hairstyle, and polished shoes, your clothing choices should portray you as someone professional who is prepared to take on the job at hand.

Your clothing must fit you well. If you can see underwear lines, your clothes are too tight. If your clothes are too big and loose, you look like you're hiding something or you are playing dress up in your mom's or dad's clothes. So clothes should fit just right. How do you tell what is a good fit? Simple: clothes should just skim your natural body gracefully.

Now that we understand fit, we must discuss that dreaded and confusing concept of Business Casual. The idea of business casual sounds great, but in reality, we now have lawyers dressing in Hawaiian shirts, shorts, and flip-flops. How confusing for a job seeker to know what to wear.

Here are the basics for anyone, male or female: if it looks like you wore it to bed or you could wear it to do yard work in, don't wear it. Even if you're applying for a landscaping or construction job, do not wear it. In today's market, you have to stand out in a positive light, not blend in.

Some of you men might love your ponytail; do you love it more than you love being employed? If you have tattoos, your options for employment are greatly expanded if you cover your tattoos at work. Piercings also limit the places you can be easily employed. Just like job seekers, employers are very conscious of the impressions they are making, and they expect your image to match theirs.

Keep your look very sharp and tailored. If you have a question about something you're wearing, then guess what the question means! It means you know deep down that something isn't looking right, so correct whatever you had that doubt about.

As you are researching the companies you're interviewing for, find out what they normally wear. Maybe they usually wear jeans and polo shirts. Guess what? You are not wearing jeans and a casual shirt to that interview. To be that polished apple, you are going to dress at least one perceived level higher than the position you're aiming for. Let the interviewer know you take this interview seriously, that you have taken your time to prepare yourself. Dress to impress them.

If you are interviewing for a very traditional major corporation, maybe in the financial industry, you're going to wear a suit. This is what I call the High-Powered Business look.

If you are interviewing with a landscaper and in an outdoor setting, well, you are not going to wear a suit, but you will probably wear what is known as a Business Casual look. Here's where a good pair of khaki pants, and a nice button-down shirt would be appropriate.

CHAPTER 12

Interview Dress Basics

Once you know the company and the position you are interviewing for, you can learn how to dress for the actual look. In some situations, you might not know which position you're actually applying for, so that is where it is essential to know what the company's mission and values are. In most situations, a suit is recommended, especially if you are anywhere near a management position.

The goal when creating an interview look is to create a very positive, polished, and professional look. Once you have that image, no matter who you are, and no matter what job you are applying for, you will glow with self-confidence. And that confidence from the inside will be reflected to the outside. You'll be dynamic, and you will stand apart. This will help you pass that two-second test. When you walk through that door, the interviewer will want to hear what you have to say. And you will be memorable—memorable because you have that "WOW!" in your look and you are radiating positive energy. Not many people have that these days, that "Wow," but you will!

Be prepared with at least two different interview outfits. It's common to be interviewed more than once, so plan for that. For men, that can be simple: have a second tie! Be ready, so if you are invited to a second interview, you won't freak out. Having your appearance all planned and knowing you look sharp raises your confidence. It's not about trying to look perfect—nobody is perfect. It is about looking like the best professional you can be. So get the idea of perfection out of your mindset; you want to look positive and professional, not perfect.

Now there is one business staple that is the easiest way to look interview-ready for any job seeker for almost any job interview—a blazer. A blazer can be very appropriate for both men and women. Even in hot climates, blazers are still great, because they add a layer of contrasts for you and create more visually interesting outfits.

Another great thing about blazers is how they have small shoulder pads which disguise that little bit of hunching over we tend to do. If your shoulders tend to slump even when you are standing perfectly straight, make sure to wear a blazer to your interview even if you live and work in a region or industry where business casual is common. The shoulder pads in the jacket will reduce the visual look of the curve in your shoulder so your shoulders look strong and steady, ready to carry the weight of responsibility.

Plus a blazer can dress up any casual look. So if you arrive to your interview and realize that everyone else is dressed more formally than you, having that blazer close at hand can be your saving grace.

When in doubt, keep your look classic, simple, and understated. It is always better to have your personality shine more than your look.

CHAPTER 13

Colors Speak. What's Your Message?

Think back for a moment to your seven-year-old self. Yes, that same self that can hinder you from being your best, most confident self right now. When you got scared, nervous, or insecure at that age, what did you do? Did you go run and hide, or did you stand and fight? Most of us ran and hid. We either hid behind our parents, in a closet, or underneath our beds. It is just human nature to experience that fight-or-flight response, and for most of us, it's flight.

We still do this today. It can be more subtle than turning around and bolting back home; it can even happen with subconscious choices that help us visually hide. Most people do this with the colors they choose to wear.

Let me ask you a question. What color or colors do you wear when going on an interview? Black? Navy? Tan? These are all very traditional business colors, but two of these can actually make you less visible and memorable to the interviewer.

HUMAN CAMOUFLAGE

I call this human camouflage. It is choosing to wear any clothing color that closely resembles your hair and skin tones. Whenever your features visually blend together, and there is little to no visual contrast in the look, then you in turn, seem to invisibly fade away.

For example, I am a fair, blonde-haired person. If I were to wear a light tan suit, my hair, skin, and clothing colors would all be relatively close together. This is human camouflage. If you have dark coloring, then the same principle applies to colors that are camouflage for you.

Human camouflage is one of those natural instincts people tend to fall back on when they are nervous, scared, or insecure—which pretty much describes any personal interview for most people. So as the name states, human camouflage, does not have you stand out, but instead, blends you into the background. This isn't good when it comes to business, let alone in an interview. So how can you not fall into the trap of human camouflage?

Add some color to your interview wardrobe! If you are purposeful about the colors you pick, you can communicate on a nonverbal level who you really are, which will help you make a positive first impression and lasting one as well. You want to be especially aware of our Western culture's color symbolism. Here are the basics on color psychology for business.

BLACK

Black, of course, is the ultimate professional color. In very traditional corporations such as the financial market, banking, accounting, or investing, black is the go-to color when interviewing for any job with authority.

RED

Red is power. Red is passion. Red is energetic. So if you are applying for a job in a powerful position, requiring lots of energy and leadership, you might want to wear a red tie or red blouse.

GREEN

Green represents calmness. It's a good way to show that you're peaceful and flexible.

BLUE

Blue represents friendliness and reliability. You can never go wrong with blue. You are going to want to wear the darker richer tones of blue, not pale baby blue, to show your professional side. Blues or greens are great for a customer service position.

PURPLE

Purple is for women only. Men should never wear purple in a business setting. For women, purple suggests creativity and spirituality, great for those in counseling or artistic careers.

AVOID PASTELS

No baby colors for men or women—no pale green, no lavender. And for men, as popular as feminine colors such as pink, yellow, and purple are, you want to avoid them completely in any place where you want to be seen as a professional. You might even have a male boss who wears them, and I still wouldn't recommend them. He's the boss, not the one being evaluated. When worn in a business setting, pastels send a subliminal cue that you are immature and not to be taken seriously. If you enjoy pastel colors, you can wear them in your casual life.

WARM OR COOL?

Once you know what message you want to send, then you choose a cool tone or a warm tone. I find that cooler blue-based colors are great for most people due to reflective color. They make your skin look rich. They deepen a tan or make pale skin look creamy. They minimize bags beneath your eyes.

In contrast, warm yellow-based colors bring out the yellows in your skin and make you look a bit jaundiced, even if your skin is very dark. If you ladies love yellow, orange, or brown, you can carry a colorful handbag, but wear the blue-based colors near your face to look youthful and refreshed.

CHOOSING COLORS PURPOSEFULLY

You can wear colors that flatter your innate coloring and also send the right message about the professional nature of the job and how you fit in. There isn't just one right color to wear for everyone. Your color choices need to be an individual, carefully considered match—balancing who you are and what the needs of the position are.

Let me give you an example. Let's say Bob is an Information Technology guy. He has worked in lower level management for many years, but never progressed past that with his previous employer. He has the skills to go forward in management, but has not had the opportunity yet. Bob is now applying for positions in the IT field at a variety of management levels. He has just gotten an interview for a middle management position at an IT company. What is he going to wear?

Well, we know Bob has management experience, and that this would be a positive step forward. So what type of characteristics does a middle management position require and what colors would suggest those characteristics?

He would need to be a good leader (black, red), yet listen to his superiors (blue), have good people skills (blue, green), and positive time management skills (blue) to name just a few. So how can Bob create a professional business look for this middle management interview?

I would suggest a black or dark gray suit with a blue or green shirt and red tie. If Bob didn't want to go so bold with his color choices, he could wear a classic white shirt, red tie, and the black or dark gray suit. These looks work well no matter what Bob's hair and skin tone is, so that is not a factor here.

Choosing the right color to wear for your interview can even help you overcome preconceptions and prejudices. I once advised a job seeker who had been told that he looked scary. I asked what he had worn. It was a black suit, with black shirt and black tie. That's a lot of black, the power color, on anyone, and he was a very large and tall African-American man. I suggested that instead, he wear a French blue button-down shirt to suggest that he's friendly and approachable, with a red tie to suggest energy and leadership. That look perfectly matched the message he really wanted to send.

Next, I'll give you some specifics about men's and women's dress. Men, you can go ahead and skip on over to Chapter 18, page 61. Ladies, let's continue on.

FOR WOMEN

CHAPTER 14

The New Rules for Women's Business Dress

Throughout history, women have been taught that only two types of women succeed in business: those who act and dress like the boys, and those who act and dress to exploit their sexy, feminine ways. These days, a highly successful woman embraces her femininity and her business savvy mind.

So ladies, I have two main rules of fashion for you: (1) Don't fall out of your top, and (2) Don't fall out of your bottom. Also, it stands to reason, don't show your midriff and don't wear anything see-through either. I know it sounds obvious. Some of you are wondering why I'm even stating it, but it is a reality. We see many women do it, from Walmart to the White House.

So sexy is out, but don't flip to the other extreme and wear boxy, masculine clothes either. Designers used to think women had to dress like men to be successful in traditionally male-dominated fields; that is no longer the case. Choose clothes that define your waist and gracefully outline your shape, embracing the balance of beauty and brains.

So what is a good interview outfit? There are a few things to consider when creating that perfect interview outfit. These days, a woman can wear pants, a skirt, or a dress to an interview. However, in large corporate interview situations, I usually suggest a two-piece skirt suit or skirt and blazer. This is a very traditional interview look for the more conservative fields and areas of the country.

When it comes to regional dress, the formality of the region needs to be considered. The East Coast and large metropolitan areas tend to be more formal in interview and business dress than the Midwest and Southwest. Also, in the sunny Southwest, it's usually considered old-fashioned and outdated to wear hosiery.

A word about hair: make sure your haircut says something. You can wear it long if you're willing to take the time to style it, or you can wear it chin-length or shorter. Those in-between lengths usually mean you can't make a decision, and they don't frame your face effectively.

A flattering cut makes a young professional woman look more mature and competent, while a great cut makes a more mature woman look younger and up-to-date. Your hairstyle contributes tremendously to having that polished and professional look.

If you choose to color your hair, be sure it's a natural color for your ethnic heritage and flatters your skin tone, and that you can maintain it impeccably.

Finally, business appropriate makeup is a must. To be successful in business, don't wear clown make-up and don't skip wearing make-up. No matter how naturally beautiful you are, you're going to need at least mascara and lip gloss to look polished and professional.

CHAPTER 15

Look Five Pounds Thinner Today

We all want to look our best, especially on the day of an interview. So looking a little bit leaner would always be a plus, right? So how can you do that? By wearing the right clothes to flatter your body type. Many women think that to look great, they'd have to change their shape, or at least their size. Maybe you're one of them. So the first key is to understand that every body type is beautiful; you just need to know how to dress it!

For almost every body shape, you'll want to define your waist. This doesn't necessarily mean to wear a belt. There are many subtler ways to define your waist, using the lines of each seam. Contouring your feminine God-given curves makes you look slimmer. When people look at you, one place they notice is the smallest width of your body. To the human eye, this narrowest part is now the size you are. We want this to be your waist. So hiding under a boxy jacket makes you look larger, whereas wearing a jacket with built-in curves will flatter your shape.

Even if you want to disguise a tummy, you can still define your waist. You can create a very beautiful and balanced look for your body type and I am proof of that.

When I got married at the age of 22, I was a cute size zero! Society loves those nonexistent sizes. Looking fun and fashionable wasn't too hard, except when clothes didn't come small enough.

Society's views of me were accepting, but that would all change for me in less than one year.

After my husband and I married, we moved from Connecticut to Louisiana to open his business. Things were stressful, with starting a new business in a new town, and remodeling the house we just moved into.

Well, shortly after that, I started to gain weight. Now I am not talking about a few pounds. I went from that size 0 to a size 12 maternity in one month! And I was not pregnant. The doctors at that time couldn't figure out what was wrong with me.

I was no longer that socially acceptable shape. I had a choice to make: let society define who I was and stop me from living fully, or decide that no matter what, I was going to do what I wanted to do. You have that choice too.

Well, years have passed since then. And yes, doctors think they have figured out what caused such a weight gain, but I still have the weight. My body shape has changed from a Maiden Silhouette to a Queen Silhouette. (I'll explain more about that next.)

Still, most people would never guess that I am the size I am. Even when I tell them, they don't believe me. It is not that they think I am a size zero, but I do know how to create looks that accentuate the positive, play down the not-so-positive and create visual contrast to make all those great parts of me pop.

Guess, what? You can have that too! And I think that is what most of us want, especially when we walk into an interview.

So we are going to discuss how to look amazing for your shape. This will be a brief overview focusing just on making that dynamic and impactful presence for an interview. Let's get started.

CHAPTER 16

Look Great in the Body You Have, Ladies

Now if you're just getting to know me, then you just learned two new terms: Maiden Silhouette and Queen Silhouette. Well, there are many different ways that people have described women's body shapes. You can be an hourglass. You can be a triangle. You can be an inverted triangle. You can be an apple or a pear. But seriously, who wants to be a pear or an inverted triangle? I have never found these labels to be positive, informative, or powerful. I see a new way to think about the different shapes our bodies come in, and I'm excited to share it with you.

I call them the four Regal Silhouettes:[SM] the Queen Silhouette, the Princess Silhouette, the Maiden Silhouette, and the Duchess Silhouette. Why? Because these titles reflect your true royal and regal heritage. Deep down, we all have a divine God-given heritage. Every woman has it.

We all tend to recognize this when we are little girls. Haven't you seen a two-year-old girl who just knows that she looks good? But as we age and mature, this connection can become weakened or lost.

Now, just because you have one Silhouette today doesn't mean that you are that Silhouette for the rest of your life. As your body changes throughout your lifetime, it could happen that your shape will change, as, well, mine did. Whether your body changes or it doesn't, you need to know that you can look great in whatever body you have at the moment. You just have to know how to dress.

Curious to find out what your Regal Silhouette is? Here is how to do it. First, ignore everything you've ever heard about body types and how other people classify the body. This has nothing to do with measuring tapes and circumferences or sizes. It does not involve the shoulders. It's very simple.

First off, face a full-length mirror, and imagine your shape as a flat silhouette. Place a yardstick under your arm, skimming the side of your bust down to your hip. If you hold the stick perpendicular to the floor, as though it's a flagpole, would it still touch the side of both your bust and hip?

Now remember, we are looking only at the front view. We are not looking at your profile. So even if you have a bit of a tummy, classify your shape by the way the stick runs alongside your bust to your hip.

What does your yardstick do? Does it touch only your hip, meaning that your hips are wider than your bust? Does it not even meet your hip, because your bust is wider than your hips? Or does your yardstick skim both your bust and your hip?

QUEEN SILHOUETTE[SM]

If your yardstick touches only your hip, meaning that your hips are wider than your bust, then you have what I call a Queen Silhouette.

A Queen Silhouette is actually the most common Silhouette in our Western society. It has been viewed as royalty throughout the years. In past centuries, other women envied these curves so much that they used to wear all types of strange contraptions to enhance the look and proportion of their curves. In today's society, we still have a few rebel Queens who are embraced by society, like Jennifer Lopez and Beyoncé. You are a true beauty.

So how can we accentuate all the positive features of a Queen Silhouette? We'll focus on the following key points: framing, defining and minimizing.

FRAME: When it comes to framing for a Queen Silhouette, you want to frame your face. Choose shirts and tops that draw the eye upward, like a "V" neck or scoop neck top. Also consider a rectangular cut like a kimono style top. This wide rectangle crossing your chest from shoulder to shoulder helps to emphasize and increase the visual width of your shoulders to keep the proportions of your hips in balance.

Another way to frame your face is to use jewelry, one of the key essentials for any woman's wardrobe. When choosing pieces, stick with earrings and necklaces. These items draw your eye upward to your face. By drawing the eye upward, we are creating a visual balance.

Choosing the right scale in your necklace is key for a Queen Silhouette. The scale of your pieces or patterns is one of the easiest ways to either make yourself look like you lost ten pounds or gained ten pounds. So when looking for the right statement necklace for you, consider your size. Are you a skinny mini? Or are you like me? Choose a necklace that is then in scale with your size. For example, a skinny mini wouldn't wear a large chunky necklace because it would overwhelm her frame, while a larger scaled necklace works well for me because I have a larger frame.

I actually have tried this before. I love jewelry and especially necklaces. Needless to say, I follow my own advice, and wear larger scaled pieces that look perfect on me. They are properly proportioned for my scale. So when I put that same necklace on a client of mine who is the skinny mini (a size double zero), it looked like we were breaking her neck. So Queens, remember to take into consideration the scale of your jewelry pieces when making your selections.

DEFINE: The next part is to visually define your waist. This does not necessarily mean tying a belt around your waist, though that is the most obvious way to do so. Defining your waist is about showing the world that you have one. Make sure that you choose garments with the curves built in—the easiest way to define your waist without using a belt. How can you tell if your clothes have built-in curves? Easy. Take out your favorite top, still on its hanger, and look at it straight on. Do the sides of the garment curve in to create a waist, or is it a box hanging there? Try choosing garments with this built-in curve to naturally define your waist without using a belt.

Now if you don't have a tummy and you like wearing belts, those can be great ways to really call attention to how small your waist is, and a belt adds a great visual layer of contrast to your overall look. And in the interview world, it just adds that finishing touch.

Remember that the human eye scans the body looking for the smallest part to define you and estimate your size. You always want that to be your waist because it is this skinny area that makes you look slimmer.

MINIMIZE: With the Queen Silhouette we aren't really trying to minimize your hips, but we are trying to create a visual balance between your hips and your bust.

We don't want to add anything in the way of clothing that will draw a person's eye to your hips and only your hips. So try to avoid three-quarter length sleeves and flared or boot-cut pants. The three-quarter length sleeve actually hits right above your hip when your arm is resting at your side, which brings the eye to your hip. Plus, those tend to make your arm look chubby.

Avoid flared or boot-cut pants because these cuts come in at the knee and flare out, therefore increasing the look of your hips. Cuts like these actually make the skinniest part of your body your knees—not your waist—which in turn makes your hips look bigger and your knees look skinnier. I have never had anyone ask me, "Can you make my knees look skinnier?" I doubt you want that look either.

DUCHESS SILHOUETTE℠

Now if your yardstick didn't even come close to skimming your hips, then you have a Duchess Silhouette. This means that your bust is wider than your hips. People pay good money to create what you have naturally been given. The hardest thing for a Duchess Silhouette is to find cuts of clothing that are flattering and stylish, but trust me—they are out there. With a Duchess Silhouette, you need to be very aware of how tops fit you. An ill-fitting top will detract most severely from your professional polish.

FRAME: As a Duchess, you need to frame your hips. I know it sounds weird. If you have a Duchess Silhouette, your goals are exactly the opposite of the Queen Silhouette's. You need to create and define your hips to help visually balance your bust. So boot-cut pants, A-line skirts, and bubble skirts are great for your shape. You can probably even pull off a straight sheath dress because your bust projects beyond any tummy you might have.

Where most people want to keep solid and dark colors on their lower region, a Duchess doesn't. The Duchess Silhouette is the body type that can pull off wearing a white pair of pants in the summertime and look great doing it. You can also wear large scaled prints or bright colored skirts and bottoms with ease. Just remember the rules: no falling out of your top or your bottom!

DEFINE: No matter what your Silhouette is, you want to define your waist. Duchesses look great in belts because that adds visual interest to the lower half of your body. You need to be aware of the scale of the belt and the position of the belt relative to your bust.

Let me give you an example. I was working with a client on a reality TV makeover show we were filming. This client is an amazing thirty-something, vivacious woman. She has a Duchess Silhouette all the way. Her bust size is an H. Needless to say, there was a disproportion between the size of her bust to the size of her hips. Most of the tops that she had didn't fit right and accentuated the size of her bust, without ever defining her waist.

By choosing clothes that defined her waist and using wider low slung belts across her hips, we were able to make her hips appear larger and her bust smaller at the same time. The width of the belt in proportion to her bust size created the visual illusion that her bust was smaller than it was. This would not have been the case if we would have used a skinny belt instead. As with the Queen Silhouette, the Duchess too needs to be aware of the scale and proportion of the accessories that you choose.

MINIMIZE: The Duchess Silhouette needs to minimize the apparent size of your bust. Wearing dark colors on top is one way to do that.

Choose tops that are sleeveless, or have long sleeves or three-quarter length sleeves.

Also try to wear earrings rather than necklaces. When wearing a necklace, the scale is critical. If your scale is off, your bust will seem larger.

Typically knit tops are out for a Duchess, but again, if you can find the right scale of a knit, you can pull that off. Lastly, choose tops without lots of ruffles or patterns or detail across the bust area. Details like these bring the eye upward and can easily look distorted and/or distracting on a Duchess Silhouette.

PRINCESS SILHOUETTE℠

If the yardstick skimmed the side of your bust and your hip, with very little definition of your waist, then you have a Princess Silhouette. (If you have a large "C" shape defining your waist, then you have a Maiden Silhouette.)

The Princess Silhouette is that long, straight, runner or supermodel body type. Again, figuring out your Regal Silhouette has nothing to with your size. You can have a Princess Silhouette if you are a size two or a size twenty-two. Size does not matter here.

The Princess Silhouette is the one that today's media is currently in love with. People like Kate Moss and Paris Hilton have the Princess Silhouette frame.

Most women want at least some curves as we grow up, so the goal for a Princess Silhouette is to create that visual illusion of womanly curves.

FRAME: Princess Silhouettes will want to frame your faces as the Queen Silhouettes do and frame your hips as the Duchess Silhouettes do. A Princess needs to add as much curve as you visually can. The more curve you can create, the more defined of a waist you will have.

DEFINE: Princesses do not naturally have much of a waist so creating the illusion is key.

MINIMIZE: Are you kidding? We don't need to minimize when it comes to the Princess or Maiden Silhouette. The Princess Silhouette actually needs to maximize every single curve you have.

MAIDEN SILHOUETTE[SM]

The Maiden Silhouette is similar to the Princess Silhouette with one huge difference. The Maiden Silhouette has your yardstick skim down the side of your bust and hip, but instead of having no defined waist, you will have a "C" shape defining your waist. You have that perfectly balanced hourglass shape that is so classically beautiful.

FRAME: Now the Maiden Silhouette can do whatever you darn well please. If you want your bust to look bigger, then frame your face and follow the advice for the Queen Silhouette. Or if you want your hips to look a bit bigger, then take the advice for framing from the Duchess.

DEFINE: Maidens naturally have that waist, so here we want to make sure that we play up the great waist you do have. Now both the Princess Silhouette and the Maiden Silhouette could have tummies. If you are a Princess or a Maiden with a bit of a tummy don't worry. Make sure to define your waist through the curve of your clothes rather than with belts.

MINIMIZE: The Maiden Silhouette has the natural balance that the Queen and Duchess Silhouette is trying to create; therefore, she does not need to minimize anything.

CHAPTER 17

Women's Interview Outfits

So now that you understand your Regal Silhouette and how to dress your shape, how do you apply that to your interview outfit?

For a Queen or Maiden Silhouette, I would suggest a straight or wide-legged pantsuit in black, gray, or navy for your interview.

A Duchess or Princess Silhouette could easily wear a skirt or a boot-cut pant in tan or even a winter white.

If you have a Queen, Maiden, or Princess Silhouette, you will want to have a great necklace to frame your face, and a pop of color in your top that reflects who you are and what the position you're applying for requires.

If you have a Duchess Silhouette, on the other hand, you will want to wear a deep-toned top. This does not necessarily mean black, but the tone of the color must be rich and deep. You would then pair your top with a great belt scaled to your size.

Throw on a great pair of heels, style your hair, apply a bit of makeup, and carry a great handbag, and you are all set to make a professional and memorable impression at your interview.

(I know that we have only briefly run through how to dress each Regal Silhouette. My other books offer more detail and illustrations for each, and explain how to dress for every occasion with your 3 Wardrobes: High-Powered Business, Business Casual, and Off-the-Clock—plus bonus Evening looks. This is just an introduction to get you off to your interview in style.)

FOR MEN

CHAPTER 18

Why Men Have It Easy

Men have it easy when it comes to dressing for success. You only have to worry about your clothes and your personal grooming—that's it. Sounds simple, doesn't it? Well, it is, and it should be, except that so many guys have no idea what they are doing.

A clean and tailored haircut and facial grooming are essential. Make sure all those hairs are in the correct place. Trim your eyebrows so that they aren't wild. No need to wax or tweeze your brows, but do make sure that you do not suffer from the unibrow or mad professor look. Also, make sure that your neck/chest area is well groomed, with no chest hair or untailored neck bursting through a fine shirt.

Proper grooming is never overrated.

Avoid cologne and aftershave for business; a little goes a long way, and many people are sensitive to it.

CHAPTER 19

Look Great in the Body You Have, Guys

Men are rectangles. It is that simple. But most guys are unaware of their body profile and don't dress to enhance their overall shape. Guys, you have seen men like this. They are the ones who are wearing short-sleeved button-up shirts that hit below their elbows.

Guys don't get a lot of accessories when dressing, so your clothing needs to be spot on, making a smashing first impression at your interview.

As with the women's body classification system, you, too, have your own. I have found that there are three main body types for men. These Regal Profiles℠ are the Prince Profile, the Knight Profile, and the Duke Profile. So which one are you?

Simply stand in from of a mirror and look at yourself. Now honestly evaluate the body you see in the mirror—not the body you used to have, or the body you want. Are your shoulders big and bulky? Are you long and lean like a runner? Or do you have a bit of a "love handle" going on?

The great thing about the male body is that you can have whatever profile you want; you just have to work at it. So if you are not happy with your body profile at this moment, then go to the gym and work out. You can change your profile. Just remember that no matter what Regal Profile you have, your clothes need to fit. Ill-fitting clothes make you look like you are playing dress up. I want you to look the part of the powerful businessperson and future employee that you are. Here's what you need to know to dress well in the body you have right now.

THE PRINCE PROFILE℠

The Prince Profile has this very long and lean shape of a runner or basketball star. Proper fitting clothes are essential for the Prince Profile. Don't believe me? Find old footage of NBA basketball players in their college years. See how they dressed off the court in their suits. Notice how those suits fit those long, lean bodies, then notice how these super stars look today in their custom-made suits. That is the difference proper fit makes for anyone with a Prince Profile.

THE KNIGHT PROFILE℠

The Knight Profile is that classic hero in the movies with wide shoulders and a highly developed upper body. Knights in today's society tend to work out to obtain their body. If you have a Knight Profile body, then you need to be aware of how shirts fit you. Your shoulders tend to be very wide, so to accommodate your shoulder and neck size, there tends to be excess fabric in the mid section. Look for European cut suits and shirts to minimize this issue.

THE DUKE PROFILE℠

The Duke Profile is similar to the Prince Profile except that the Duke has a bit of a "love handle." It is very common for men to carry your weight in your stomachs, especially as you age. The key is to minimize the look of your stomach and create the illusion of greater height.

Defining your shoulder through blazers is one key. And you want to minimize bulky fabric around your waist. So no double or even front-pleated pants for you—only flat front pants. Have your pants tailored to eliminate any excess fullness in the leg and seat areas.

Also the Duke Profile tends to overcompensate for the width of the stomach by just purchasing a larger shirt. If you are going to do this, then only wear long-sleeved shirts. This will minimize the fact that the shirt is not fitting you well, and the long sleeve will visually minimize the look of your stomach.

Too many men tuck the waist of their pants underneath their bellies in an effort to disguise it. Well, this actually exaggerates the shape because the color of the shirt lengths the torso, visually shortening the legs, and emphasizing the entire girth of the belly. It is best for pants to sit at the natural waist—not nerdy high-wasted either.

If at all possible, Dukes should invest in a good tailor. It will make a world of difference for you.

CHAPTER 20

Men's Business Dress

Guys, you are so lucky. The rules for men are much easier than fashion for women. Plus great clothes are not hard to find. Because your styles don't change and you don't need many different clothes, invest in the best quality you can afford. Here are the basics for any businessman's wardrobe: a nice suit, blazer, pants, shirts, and a great pair of shoes. That's it.

Let's be honest, most men don't care about the clothes on their backs. But clothes do matter, so why not choose pieces that create a commanding presence instead of human camouflage? Guys, don't you want to turn heads when you enter those company doors, and then again when you enter the interview room? I think anybody does, and I think that deep down, men especially do.

Now there are many options in today's market where personal style comes into play, but when it comes to a guy's personal style and his business style, those are still two separate things. Yes, we want to know who you really are, but we also need to know that you are a professional businessman, and that can be two different things. You may love Hawaiian-print shirts, but don't you dare wear them to an interview! If you have that fun quirky side, then save it for your home life. Your interview dress should always say, "I am a business professional."

So how can you do that? It is really simple. You don't get too many choices, Guys, so listen up. You have slacks, long-sleeved button-up shirts, maybe a Polo shirt for a manual labor interview, ties, and shoes. Out of all of that, your ties are the only way you can express your personality and creativity, and match the job's qualities as well. So what should you wear for an interview?

Well, most business environments wear business casual to some degree. If that's the case for your interview, then a traditional three-piece suit is not necessary, but you do need some pieces.

Your list is much smaller than a businesswoman's wardrobe, so it's even more essential that each piece be high quality. The quality is immediately obvious, and because you have fewer choices, each piece should withstand many uses. This makes you look great, creates that positive first impression, and saves you from having to shop very often.

PANTS

Make sure to have a great pair of slacks that are universal. A universal or neutral pair of pants is a great way for a guy to go, and these same pants can be used for multiple interviews. These pants should be flat front, in black, gray, dark brown, or tan. A tailored pin stripe is acceptable, but no crazy zoot suit stripes.

Make sure that your pants are long enough when you bend your legs and sit. Pants that are obviously too short make you appear as a little boy rather than as the successful businessman. A baggy, droopy pant is never professional.

SHIRTS

Wear a long-sleeved, button-up shirt. Short-sleeved button-up shirts are for little boys. Even in hot, more casual climates, go long. If you're warm, you can roll up your shirtsleeves.

Now your shirts should fit you. Make sure that the shoulder seam meets just where your arm and torso meet or slightly below that line. Solid color shirts are the most business acceptable. You can also work with a small stripe, but you must be careful. Stripes can begin to look too collegiate, as though you're barely out of school rather than being the experienced professional you are.

Choose a color that reflects one of the attributes that this job requires. A French blue shirt is great for almost all men, because most jobs require friendliness. Another option would be a green shirt—not soft green, but a rich forest green. If you want to try the boldness of red, stick with a dark maroon or cranberry; it's a great power color.

Now how do you create a dynamic look that really says, Wow? That's with your tie.

TIES

Most guys nowadays do not wear ties. They think, "Oh it is too much; it is too fussy." But the right tie can really help you create a commanding and lasting presence. It is the only thing that can set you apart in a positive way.

Classic business ties that announce you're professionally, financially successful are solid color ties, and ties with a small repeating pattern. More wild ties like stripes, paisley patterns, and especially cartoons, suggest youth and immaturity.

Men's acceptable business colors hold true with ties. Pastels and feminine patterns send a subliminal cue that you are immature and not to be taken seriously. If you enjoy pastel colors, wear them in your casual life.

So let's say you have that red shirt and black slacks. What color tie would you wear with it? You could wear a black solid tie if you wanted to. This would create a professional, almost hard look.

If you wanted to be a little more approachable, what about a blue tie, and if possible, one with a small symmetrical pattern that repeats red and yellow in it. That is a very classic look. The blue in the tie sends a friendly message, and that small symmetrical pattern says you are good with money. Who wouldn't want you on their team if they think you are good with money?

SUITS/BLAZERS

All guys should have a well-fitting blazer in a classic three or two-button style. Keep it in the car with you for any type of white-collared job.

Try to avoid double-breasted suits; they just add fullness around your torso, and most guys don't need or want to look heavier than they really are.

Most off-the-rack suits are boxes, with the torso as wide as the shoulders, which isn't the kind of rectangle I meant. That is not proper fit. A well-tailored blazer will last you for ten years or even more, so it's an important investment.

ALL THE REST

I know I shouldn't have to say it, but I must. Dark matching socks and polished shoes are needed to complete your powerful interview look. When it comes to shoes, there are so many classic shoes, it is hard to purchase the wrong style. Slip-on can be seen as more mature than a lace up, but as long as they are black or brown, clean and classic, it doesn't matter.

The most important thing is taking the time to polish them. Polished shoes show self-respect and attention to detail, and they make your investment last longer.

CHAPTER 21

Overcoming Preconceptions

I know some of you larger guys can have a hard time balancing your look; you want to look impressive as a professional, without going so far as to appear intimidating. To overcome this, you might actually wear colors that are not so powerful because you already have that naturally powerful presence. So maybe instead of wearing that bold red shirt, you wear a blue one showing friendliness. You need to be able to read how other people perceive you and take the environment into consideration.

(Not sure how others perceive you? Make sure to check out the upcoming chapter, "Leave Your Baggage Behind.")

The same point holds true for gentlemen who are a bit shorter. Maybe you are always trying to appear stronger, taller, and bigger. If this is the case for you, then wearing power colors is a great way to create a more dynamic and powerful look, but you still need to be careful about how you wear power colors. You still want to seem friendly and approachable, because sending a message of power and aggressiveness might not be the right first impression for you either.

That's all you need, Guys. You're almost ready to go out there and ace that interview.

PART THREE

CHAPTER 22

Leave Your Baggage Behind

You have the interview—Yeah!

Before you go, you need to have a serious one-on-one heart-to-heart chat with yourself. If necessary, do what one of the first grade teachers did at my elementary school, and drag yourself off by your ear for a serious talking to.

This is the time that you need to confront, come clean, and deal with all those fears and insecurities that you still have inside of you. If you don't, these issues won't go away, and will come back to haunt you, and even hurt you when you are the most stressed out and the most nervous you can be—which is what a job interview tends to be for most of us.

So how do you know what your issues are? I know there are some of you out there saying, "I have no issues. I am sleek, I'm smooth, and I close the deal."

Really? Well, sleek, smooth, and closing the deal most likely comes off as phony, insecure, and a whole bunch of smoke. The main point of a job interview is for you to genuinely show the interviewer who you are, and for them to find out whether you are a good fit for the company. They want to see who you are today—not who you were, or who you think everybody wants you to be.

So where are your hang-ups? We all have them. If you already know some of them write them down on a sheet of paper.

THE FLASHBACK

Now let's go back to your last interview. How did it go? I don't mean overall. I mean specifically. With paper and pen near by, close your eyes, and replay that entire day of your last interview in your head. Even if this interview didn't land you a job, what happened at your last interview?

Start with the résumé. Remember, eyes closed, as soon as you've finished this paragraph. What did your résumé look like? Were you proud of it? Was it honest and truthful? Did it reflect you in a positive light? Or did you feel like the person on the paper wasn't who you are?

Write down how you were feeling. Were you excited, proud, scared, confident, lost, or something else?

Now fast forward to the point where you got the call or e-mail to come in for an interview. How were you feeling? Excited, nervous, or not interested at all?

Write down how you were feeling.

Make sure to mention why you were feeling the way you were. Maybe you didn't want that job because it wasn't your dream job, but you applied because of a sense of obligation. Or maybe you were just stressed and tired from job searching, then you felt overwhelmed with how quickly they wanted to meet with you.

The why is always crucial. So don't rush this exercise. If the why doesn't pop out at you immediately, take your time. Sit in a quiet place with no distractions and sit and think back and re-experience that time in your life.

Let's flash back again to the day of the interview. How did you feel? Did you feel prepared or did it seem like you were forgetting something? Did you know exactly what you were going to wear and bring to the interview, right down to how you were going to transport the copies of your résumés, protecting them from finger smudges?

How were you feeling, and what were you doing before the interview? Was it life as usual, with the interview just a casual errand to run? Or were you prepared, relaxed, and focused on the task at hand, the interview? Write about what you were doing and how you were feeling in the hours before the interview.

Now remember traveling to the interview. Were you running late, on time, or early? Were you nervous and scared, or cool, calm, and collected? Were your hands sweating or your arms shaking ever so slightly? Write how you were feeling as you were traveling to your interview.

Now remember being there. You were sitting in the company lobby, waiting. Who was around you? Were there other people interviewing for the same position, or was it just you sitting there?

How were you sitting? Straight or slouched? Were your arms folded or were you sitting reading a magazine? Were you making small talk or sitting quietly, staring into space? Were you smiling or frowning? What were the thoughts running through your head?

You see the interviewer walking towards you. What does he or she see when looking at you?

They are close now. They call your name, you stand up, and do what? How do you gather up your personal belongings? How do you shake hands?

Stop and remember what you thought about their handshake. How were you feeling?

Picture yourself in your mind's eye. How do you look? Go beyond your clothes. How is your body positioned? Are you standing tall or slouched over ever so slightly? Write that all down.

You are in the interview room. Are you alone with one interviewer or is this a panel interview? How does the interviewer look? What are you thinking and why?

They ask you to take a seat. You sit. How are you sitting? Where are your hands? Ladies, where do you put your purse? Do you know you have turned your cell phone off, or are you worrying because you can't remember whether you did or not?

The interviewer asks the first question. What is it?

How do you respond?

Now be in that moment, as you are responding. What is the reaction on the interviewer's face, and what is your response?

The interview continues. How has the mood of the room shifted? Do you feel like you are connecting with your interviewer, or is it still cold and distant? Are you smiling? Are you being yourself? What is the facial reaction of the interviewer as you go through the interview process? Does the expression remain the same, or do they crack a smile every once in a while?

As the interview is wrapping up, what do you say? How are you feeling? What does the interviewer say? Does it seem genuine? Or does it sound absentminded, as though the interviewer is off to the next interview already?

Write everything down. Answer all the questions as completely as possible. Do any other emotions or feelings come up for you?

In that moment, how did you feel the interview went?

Did you end up getting the job?

THE BIRD'S EYE VIEW

Now let's review what you experienced and see how we can use the positive and not-so-positive aspects of this memory to help you have a more powerful and positive experience the next time you interview.

Don't view your answers from the internal perspective of the person experiencing the situation. Instead, become a detective, objectively looking at the feelings, body language, and overall clues. View it objectively, as if the responses you had are all valid and logical.

For example, it is reasonable to be nervous going on an interview. However, it is illogical not to prepare for the interview when you are feeling nervousness and you have the time to prepare. In this example, I would question the job seeker. Are you not subconsciously sabotaging the interview by not preparing, and then minimizing your nervousness?

You want to be looking for any patterns in behavior, feelings, or body language that don't match up to how a successful interview would go.

Another example of this may be that you were frowning with your arms crossed in the waiting room and throughout the interview. This would suggest that you are unhappy and that you don't want to be there. You just want to get through the interview and go home, almost like you are only there under some sense of obligation.

Now if the feelings you wrote down to accompany those actions included being happy, excited, and well prepared, then there is a major disconnect between what your actions were and what you felt like. Do you see that? It is in this disconnect that self-sabotage could be playing a big role in your interviews.

Ready to start evaluating your last interview? Okay, here we go.

First off, look at everything that led up to being in the waiting room of the company. What did you do to prepare? Did you honestly do your best, or was it a bit haphazard? What were the emotions you wrote down? And most importantly why were you feeling that way?

Now look at what you wrote about how you were feeling and behaving while you were waiting. If you were feeling nervous or negative in the preparation stage, did you do anything to change those feelings for the interview?

If you had been watching yourself sitting there in the waiting room, what would you be thinking about that person? Does that perception (of how you would view yourself as an onlooker) match how you were really feeling? Do your actions and emotions match up?

Go through the rest of the interview just like this, evaluating whether or not your actions match how you were feeling. Use the reactions of the interviewer to help you see from a third party's perspective about how you came across in that instance.

I know that evaluating yourself like this can be a bit strange the first few times, but understanding how you behave in a real interview is crucial to overcoming any self-sabotage and getting the job you want. (For more resources to help you become more efficient at this process, visit HelloJobBook.com.)

As you go through the job searching process, create an interview journal. And after every interview, write down all the things we just discussed. If viewed objectively, this will help you pinpoint any interview mistakes you may be making. You will begin to see patterns emerge, and once you are aware of them, you can correct those if necessary. You will no longer have that nagging question, "Was it me or them?" after your interviews.

CHAPTER 23

The View from the Other Side of the Desk

Before we go any farther, let's take a moment and look at the other side of the same interview coin. There you are, the job seeker on one side, and then there is the potential employer on the other side. By viewing this through the employer's eyes, you can really begin to see what they are looking for in their next employee.

I know some of you have heard this, but do you really try to see it that way? We all know the old saying, "The customer is always right," but how many service workers truly treat the customer as if they are always right? Not too many. So when you are job searching and researching the company, ask yourself, "What do they want and what do they need?" Sometimes those can even be two different things.

Coming from the employer's side, I understand how hard it can be to find quality employees. A quality employee is not necessarily one who has lots of degrees or education. A quality employee to me is a willing employee, one who is willing to stretch and bend with the company, to try new things and be open to the opportunities at hand.

Not many small to medium companies, or even large companies for that matter, have every single thing planned out a year in advance. Things come up, and companies need employees who are willing to come along and step up to the new challenges at hand. So be open and willing to do your absolute best for your future employer. And if your heart is already there for the company you are interviewing for, let them know.

Most companies don't want to keep rehiring people, so commitment and loyalty are essential. I know it sounds obvious, doesn't it? But it isn't. I have had employees come to work hours late, not show up at all, and decide that they were going to rewrite the rules to better suit themselves. Let me just say it clearly. None of this is acceptable. This isn't viewed as independence; it is viewed as arrogance and unwillingness to do as asked. Show that you are committed and loyal by showing up on time and putting in a true full day's worth of work. Don't try to skip out a few minutes early or start powering down the computers before the end of the day. Be willing to inconvenience yourself for the good of the company.

And when it comes to loyalty, be loyal to the company, not to your manager. Don't take sides in any office gossip. Remember you are not there to gossip; you are there to help the company succeed at its mission.

Lastly, do not bring personal issues to work. As employers, we all understand that personal issues arise. Make sure to have them minimally impact your time at work and the quality of your work. Any quality company will appreciate your sincere heart when you put their needs above your own. This not only helps you have a long and happy career with your company, but I wouldn't be surprised to see it lead to numerous promotions. By having your mind off yourself and your mind on the company's needs, you will definitely be an ideal and greatly appreciated employee.

Most employers want more than a warm body to fill the space. Employers want people who are committed to the same causes, goals, and purposes that they espouse. They want people who go above and beyond, and who don't whine and complain. Companies want people who care, listen, understand, apply, and do. They want people who want to work because they love the work, not just because they want a paycheck. Companies want people who care about the company and the people they serve or help. Companies want people who are flexible, who don't complain that this or that isn't in their job description. By having a servant's heart, a genuine heart for helping, you will be a company's dream employee.

So how can this help you now as you are job seeking and interviewing?

First off, if this is your true nature, let the interviewer know by your past job performance. Most likely, the idea of serving the company before yourself is something you must have already been doing. If so, mention something in your job history that shows that.

If this has not been your past nature, admit to it and let them know that you are truly willing to change. Now do this only if you are really willing to make the commitment necessary. Again, as I stated earlier, lying doesn't get you anywhere. Make your new personal company motto, "How can I help you, the company, today?"

CHAPTER 24

Want a No-Panic Interview?

You're ready to make a great impression with your personal image and résumé, and your attitude, but what are you going to say and how will you say it? You have an interview, and you already know that the interviewer is not your enemy, but neither is this person your long lost best friend. So, what do you do? Say? Act? Help!

Well, first off, it is okay to breathe. It is normal to feel nervous. You want this to go well. You want to hurry up and find your job and get started. So the best way to put your mind at ease is to prepare. The more you prepare, the more comfortable and natural you feel, and the more likely you'll be to make a great impression. So be purposeful and practice!

Practice how you walk into the room. Are your shoulders back? Are you calm, cool and collected?

It's often been estimated that 93% of all communication is non-verbal. And 30% of nonverbal communication is in the tone, pitch, rate of speech, and the rhythm of your voice. Women's voices in particular tend to rise when we are nervous, and men tend to be annoyed by that, so ladies, practice very consciously to maintain your usual pitch when you practice your interview skills.

There is only so much time allotted for your interview. It won't take you long to make a positive impression and get your point and personality across. Practice what you are going to say, using a mirror.

I know it sounds weird, but it really helps. Look at yourself as you speak. Be conscious about looking yourself in the eye. A lot of people think they look others in the eye, yet they don't.

Rehearse simple questions like the most common and ominous one, "Tell me about yourself!" Speak with intention and purpose. Practice pausing to think instead of filling a space with "umms and aahs." The more you practice, the more comfortable you will be during your interview. This isn't about having a speech memorized. Just be comfortable talking about your experience, your education, and how you can help the company.

Also make sure your talking points have a beginning, middle, and end. If the interviewer wants to know how you achieved something at your former job, make sure the story fully explains how you did it, what was the outcome and how you can help their company. Make sure to hit all points in a concise manner.

Let me give you an example. Let's say an interviewer is asking me, "Alison, I see on your résumé that at your former job, you increased the revenue for people's companies. Can you tell me more about that?"

I could say, "Well, yeah, like, I help people dress well and that just makes them more money. A lot of my personal clients are business owners and they always look good. They tend to like their new looks. We work on their hair, clothes, and makeup for women. We also do interiors."

Or I could say, "Yes, the focus of my company, 3 Impressions, is to help business professionals increase their bottom line, by establishing a consistently positive impression with their clientele. We do this by helping the company reflect their personal mission in both their employees' personal image and in their workspace design. On average, we increase the companies' sales significantly within the first six months. I can easily apply those skills to your company by helping your staff and workspace reflect your desired image for your business."

Can you see the difference in the two responses? Both answers actually answer the interviewer's question, but the first response rambles. The second response is concise and fully answers the interviewer's questions with a beginning, middle, and end.

(For more examples and resources, visit HelloJobBook.com, and see the special DVD offer in the back of the book.)

You'll probably be invited to ask a few questions, so be prepared for that as well. This is not the place to ask about benefits and vacation days. If you've researched the company, then you know quite a bit about the corporate culture, projects, charitable causes, and future direction. It's a great place to shine, because your research will show. Here's a chance to clarify something you're genuinely interested in and find out if the job is a good fit for you.

CHAPTER 25

Is Your Body Language Ratting You Out?

Besides what you say during your interview, your body is talking, too. You can be saying how great and confident you are, but your body could be giving your true feelings away by the body language you are sending out. Human Resources professionals are trained to read body language so be aware of not only what you say, but how your body is behaving.

Your posture is as important to your appearance as your clothing. Many people nowadays tend to slump—including me when I am not being aware of my posture! We just don't sit up straight anymore. So the simple act of standing straight and sitting straight is critical.

When we don't sit up straight, we are cuing our subconscious that we are giving in, that we cannot take the weight of the world. And in a job interview, that is not what an employer wants to see. They want to see someone who can carry a load and lighten their burdens. This is all subconscious, so it is very subtle, but it does affect everybody—some more than others. You never know who will be interviewing you and you want them to listen to what you have to say and have your body language back up the words you are speaking.

Be aware that if you tend to cross your arms, you give the subconscious cue that you are closed off and not really interested. So remember to have open body language; as you meet the interviewer, stand up straight, with no crossed legs or arms. The same holds true when you are seated during the interview. Place your arms at your side. And ladies, do NOT put your purse in your lap. This gives off a similar closed body language cue.

Also, if you cross your legs, you're likely to start kicking with it, showing your inner nervousness. So keep your feet flat on the floor and sit up straight, indicating that you are involved and interested.

American business etiquette requires a firm handshake. Make sure that when you shake hands that your hand is vertical; do not turn it flat or take your left hand and use it to cover your shaking hand. This shows that you are dominant. In an interview situation, you must be aware of these subtle cues. All of this information may be new to you, but it isn't new to most interviewers.

The best tip of all that I can give you is that people hire and befriend people they relate to. They must view you as an equal. Even if you don't feel like their equal, mimic their body language, but always do so respectfully. Be their respectful, perceived equal.

What other nonverbal communications do you need to remember on the big interview day?

1. Don't chew gum, only mints.

2. If you are interviewing in a medical or educational environment, wearing perfume or cologne is a no-no. For all other work environments, make sure to use it sparingly. Many people are allergic to or simply annoyed by scented products, so be considerate. Strong fragrances give the impression that you need a lot of attention and affirmation.

3. When you go to your interview, take your two résumés, and your list of references.

CHAPTER 26

Mouth Don't Fail Me Now

We have all had those moments where we inserted one big foot in mouth, or we got so tongue-tied, we couldn't even speak. The more you've practiced, the more articulate and confident you will be, and the more you'll be able to relate to your interviewer in a natural way.

The interview is the only time you have left to sell yourself. You presented yourself well on paper in your résumés, and you can certainly do it in person now. Be prepared to mention every positive attribute that you have that is relevant to the job at hand. There is no need to mention that you are great with kids, if the job is working strictly with adults.

Before your interview, practice answering the sample questions below. I can't say it enough. This will help you cultivate quick and concise answers for you to use on your interview. The objective is not to have you memorize your answers. The goal of this exercise is twofold: one, to help you get comfortable talking about yourself, and two, to remember all the wonderful strengths and attributes you have so you can go in with an appropriate level of confidence.

Let's begin with meeting your interviewer. Make sure you know and use your interviewer's name. Call the person Mr. X or Ms. Y unless you're invited to use the first name.

If you have a business card or calling card, exchange business cards with your interviewer. This way you will easily have their contact information to follow up at a later date. Now, do not use your old company's business cards with their contact information scratched out and your personal information hand written in. This will not make a positive impression for you.

Be completely honest about your education and assets, and any liabilities such as an arrest or termination. Do not blame your former employer for everything. If you had a disagreement and that lead to your termination, state that and move on. Do not bad mouth your former employer or former coworkers.

If you are asked about the salary you are looking for, say that you are open. By doing this, you don't limit yourself to what you think you are worth or allow a few dollars to stop you from landing your dream job. Only bring up money if the interviewer does. Otherwise you give off the impression that you are only there for a paycheck, not a career.

We all know that one of the first questions asked is a variation on, "Tell me a little bit about yourself."

In your answer, make sure to mention your job history, education, and any volunteer work. Make sure to focus your answer to highlight why you fit the job you are interviewing for, not just any job in general.

Another question that always pops is, "Why do you want this position?" or "Why do you feel like you are qualified for this job?" The best way to answer these questions is by citing specific examples in your history on how you have shown the skills you need for this new job. Make sure to mention that you are willing to learn. Again be honest. If you aren't willing to learn, don't say it just because you think they want to hear it.

At the end of the interview, always thank the person, and if you are interested in the position, say so. Don't say corny things like, "When do I start?" Statements like that are too pushy and can turn the interviewer off of you immediately.

Ask if there is anything else they would like to see from you: more references, certain types of identification, or more examples of your work? If you are looking for a long-term career, let them know. You need to be as helpful, open, and honest as you can be.

Before you go, ask when they will be making a decision. This way you know when to contact them.

The last step is follow up. Send the interviewer a handwritten thank you note with your card in it. If you only have their e-mail, make sure to send them a thank you e-mail. In both cases, make sure to do this within 24 hours of the interview.

Also make sure to mention specific details. For example if the interviewer mentioned that they have a dog named Buddy, you could say something like, "I just want to thank you again for your time. I hope you and Buddy have an amazing weekend together. I look forward to speaking with you soon." Little personal touches like these show that you care and that you were listening.

If you are sending a thank you card, make sure to put your calling card inside as an added reminder of who you are. If you are sending an e-mail, make sure that your e-mail signature includes a professional business headshot of you.

The goal and purpose of the thank you note is not only to genuinely thank the interviewer, but to get you back on their radar screen again. So by adding professional, personal touches like the calling card or the picture in your e-mail signature, the interviewer can remember who you are, without confusing you with anyone else they interviewed. Little acts like these help to create a positive, permanent, and lasting impression of you.

Now if the interviewer said that they would be making a decision in two weeks, and the two weeks arrive without any news, I would give them a call just to check in and ask whether they have made their decision. When calling, always make sure to ask if this is a good time to talk, and ask them how are they doing?

If they have filled the position and you were not it, then you thank them for their time and ask them to keep you in mind for any other positions that may become available. By adding just that little bit in, about other positions, it may just jog the interviewer's mind about another position that is available or may be coming available shortly.

The old saying is true: "You can catch more flies with honey than with vinegar." So if your interview didn't go as you have planned, stay nice. Being positive is the only thing that is going to move you forward.

CHAPTER 27

Find Your Job Sooner

Lastly, and most importantly, you must stay positive! "A Happy Heart makes the face cheerful but heartache crushes the spirit." (Proverbs 15:13) I know that some days, it can be easier said than done. But in a tight job market, or at any time, who wants to hire someone who is negative or depressed? Would you want to work with a Negative Betty or Depressed Donald day in and day out? I didn't think so.

So be yourself, and be your best, most positive self. Don't talk negatively about how your life is, about former coworkers, or bosses. If you are negative or just waiting for the next best thing, you won't attract that quality employer you are looking for. Remember, you want to start these new work relationships on a positive note. We hope they'll love you and want to keep you around for years and years to come.

Best of all, a positive attitude helps YOU. Not every interview leads to a job, and not getting the job is not necessarily about you. Finding the right job is like playing that childhood Concentration game where you find the two matching pictures. The employers are looking for people like themselves to fill their needs, while you are looking for a place to best use your gifts and talents. Sometimes, no matter how perfect the job looks on paper, and no matter how good you look on paper, it just isn't a match. Your match is looking for you. So stay positive, if only for yourself, and you will be amazed at where that positive attitude will lead you.

Focus on how you can best serve your future employer. Do your research, dress with purpose, and be positive, and you will find the job for you. Believe in yourself.

Remember you only need one job!

CHAPTER 28

Hello, Job, at Last!

When you dress for the first day on the job, dress to impress, just as you did on the job interview. Remember, you are building your reputation every day. If you've been honest about your qualifications and whether the job is a good match for you, you're going to keep making a positive impression on everyone you work with, furthering your career success for many years to come.

EMPLOYEE TRAINING CAMP CHECKLIST

In case you read straight through without completing each suggestion, this can remind you of some ways to strengthen your job seeking skills.

PSYCH UP

- ❑ Speak only positive things about yourself and your future job. Remind yourself that you only need one job, and your match is looking for you.
- ❑ Do the "Who Are You?" exercise. Know what you are qualified to do, and why.
- ❑ Stay positive and make a positive impression everywhere you go.

SUIT UP

- ❑ Set up voice mail and check it at least daily.
- ❑ Prepare short and long résumés ready to be tailored for specific openings.

- ❑ Prepare list of references.
- ❑ Does your profession typically require something special? Portfolio, identification card, etc.
- ❑ Get a great haircut.
- ❑ Be neatly groomed with good hygiene.
- ❑ Prepare professional wardrobe to look the part of the job you want. Be sure your clothes fit well, flatter your body type, and send the right message by the colors and styles you wear.
- ❑ Cover any tattoos or piercings.
- ❑ Get a professional headshot taken.

SHOW UP

- ❑ Be able to explain who you are and what your goals are in 30 seconds or less.
- ❑ Practice mock interview questions, paying attention to your voice and your body language as well as your words.
- ❑ Stay positive!

GAME DAY CHECKLIST

You've been invited to an interview! Congratulations! First off, stop and breathe. You will do fine, especially if you took some of the advice found in this book. Below is a checklist for you to run through before your interview so you'll know you're thoroughly prepared.

PSYCH UP

- ❑ Know that your match is looking for you. And prepare for your interview in the spirit of helping the interviewer find the right person for that job, whether it's you or not.
- ❑ Know what you are qualified to do—and why.

- ❑ Be able to explain who you are and what your goals are in 30 seconds or less.
- ❑ Prepare to make a positive impression.
- ❑ Breathe deeply, smile, and say, "Hello, Job!"

SUIT UP

- ❑ Research the company, its mission and values statements, and what their current projects are.
- ❑ Tweak your résumés to highlight the skills and experiences that qualify you for this opening.
- ❑ Did the company ask you to bring anything special? Portfolio, identification card, etc.
- ❑ Do you know who you are meeting with, and how to get there? Do you have the phone number just in case you get lost?
- ❑ Be neatly groomed with good hygiene.
- ❑ Wear your carefully chosen interview outfit.
- ❑ Cover any tattoos.

SHOW UP

- ❑ Go to your interview dressed to impress and radiating happiness.
- ❑ Take your résumés and list of references.
- ❑ Be honest and friendly. Remember you and the interviewer are on the same team.
- ❑ Always follow up with a thank you card and/or call.
- ❑ Stay positive, certain that you'll find your job.
- ❑ Land your job and love it.

Remember,

You are not alone.

You are enough.

You are fully capable.

You are wonderful just the way that you are.

You are loved.

"For I know the plans I have for you, declares the Lord, plans to prosper you and not to harm you, plans to give you hope and a future."

— Jeremiah 3:13 NLT

About the Author

Image consultant and interior designer Alison Craig designs success. She is the founder of 3 Impressions, and also volunteers with the Phoenix First Workforce satellite office; their team has been so successful in helping job seekers get hired, their office has become a model for the program.

While working toward her interior design degree, Alison worked at a high-end boutique serving professional women. She has studied with image consultants and makeup artists around the world. It was only natural that Alison would synergize these two worlds of image and interior design into a new concept for image services. She is out to help you express your goals, personality, and originality in your personal image and office design so you can achieve your dreams. Learn more at 3Impressions.com.

Free Offer: Alison Craig's Interview Skills DVD

As my way of helping you say, "Hello, Job" sooner, I'd be happy to send you my Interview Skills DVD, worth $32, for only $9 shipping and handling. No phone or website orders will be accepted for this special offer. Fax this completed order form to 866-278-0628.

Please print clearly and completely.

Name ______________________________

Address ______________________________

____

City ______________________________ State ____________

Zip Code ____________ Birthday (Month/Day) ____________

Phone ______________________________

E-mail ______________________________

Make checks payable to 3 Impressions or charge: ❑ Visa ❑ MC

Credit Card no. ______________________________

Exp date ______________________________

Signature ______________________________